ABDO Publishing Company

BUGS!
Grasshoppers

Kristin Petrie

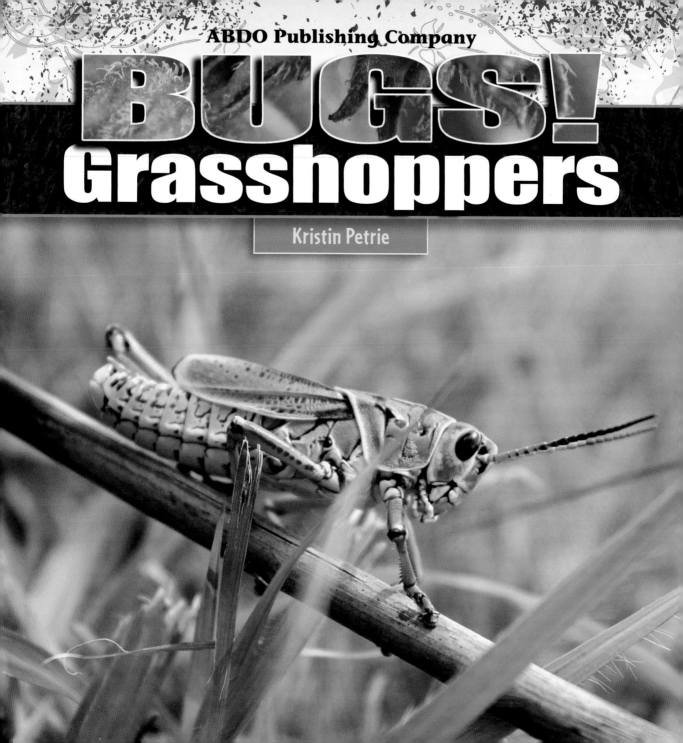

visit us at
www.abdopublishing.com

Published by ABDO Publishing Company, 8000 West 78th Street, Edina, Minnesota 55439. Copyright © 2009 by Abdo Consulting Group, Inc. International copyrights reserved in all countries. No part of this book may be reproduced in any form without written permission from the publisher. The Checkerboard Library™ is a trademark and logo of ABDO Publishing Company.

Printed in the United States.

Cover Photo: iStockphoto
Interior Photos: Alamy pp. 18, 23, 28; Andy Williams/CritterZone.com pp. 12–13, 17; AP Images
     p. 22; Corbis pp. 27, 29; Getty Images pp. 10, 12, 24; Glenn McCrea/CritterZone.com p. 15;
     iStockphoto pp. 1, 11, 19, 21, 25; Mark Plonsky pp. 5, 8–9; Photo Researchers p. 7

Series Coordinator: BreAnn Rumsch
Editors: Megan M. Gunderson, BreAnn Rumsch
Art Direction & Cover Design: Neil Klinepier

Library of Congress Cataloging-in-Publication Data

Petrie, Kristin, 1970-
  Grasshoppers / Kristin Petrie.
      p. cm. -- (Bugs!)
  Includes index.
  ISBN 978-1-60453-069-8
  1. Grasshoppers--Juvenile literature. I. Title.

QL508.A2P48 2009
595.7'26--dc22

                                    2008004792

Contents

Great Grasshoppers

Run! Hide! The orthopterans are coming! These sound like lines from a science fiction or horror movie. In fact, these creatures have been featured in several scary movies!

Orthopterans can seem like aliens or monsters. These creatures have horns, sharp jaws, and five eyes. They have large legs and can jump long distances. And they make eerie noises, especially at dusk.

In addition to their frightful appearance, some orthopterans fly in enormous swarms. These swarming insects darken the sky and make a **deafening** noise.

Then, they land like a blanket on fields and crops. When these orthopterans take off, the fields are bare! The flying, noisy creatures have eaten everything in sight. Have you guessed what orthopterans are? They are grasshoppers!

The word Orthoptera means "straight winged." This phrase perfectly describes most orthopterans.

What Are They?

Grasshoppers are insects. Like all insects, they belong to the class Insecta. Within this class, grasshoppers are part of the order Orthoptera.

The order Orthoptera is very large. For this reason, orthopterans are divided into two **suborders**. These groups are based on the length of their antennae, known as horns. Orthopterans from the suborder Caelifera have short horns. Orthopterans from the suborder Ensifera have long horns.

Katydids are long-horned grasshoppers. Within their suborder, they belong to the family Tettigoniidae. True grasshoppers have short horns. These grasshoppers belong to the family Acrididae.

Each species of grasshopper has a two-word name called a binomial. A binomial combines the genus with a descriptive name, or epithet. For example, a common field grasshopper's binomial is *Chorthippus brunneus*.

Grasshoppers come in many shapes and sizes. Some are brightly colored, while others blend into their surroundings.

THAT'S CLASSIFIED!

Scientists use a method called scientific classification to sort the world's living organisms into groups. Eight groups make up the basic classification system. In descending order, they are domain, kingdom, phylum, class, order, family, genus, and species.

The phrase "Dear King Philip, come out for goodness' sake!" may help you remember this order. The first letter of each word is a clue for each group.

Domain is the most basic group. Species is the most specific group. Members of a species share common characteristics. Yet, they are different from all other living things in at least one way.

Body Parts

Like all insects, grasshoppers have six legs. They also have an exoskeleton to protect their insides. This outer shell is made of a tough material called chitin. Grasshoppers also have three body **segments**. These are the head, the thorax, and the abdomen.

A grasshopper's segmented body starts with a large head. Two bulging compound eyes dominate the head. Compound eyes are made of hundreds of connected lenses. They allow grasshoppers to see in all directions. In addition, three smaller eyes sit between the grasshopper's black, bulging ones. These smaller eyes are called ocelli. They can only detect light and dark.

The grasshopper's head also houses its strong mouth. This mouth is necessary for eating large plant parts. Sharp jaws stick out of the mouth. These jaws tear and chew tough leaves and stems. In front of the jaws are two pairs of feelers called palpi. These help the grasshopper taste its food.

You use your tongue to taste food. A grasshopper uses its four palpi instead.

Next on the head are the antennae, or horns. Antennae have an important job. They gather information through touch and smell. The antennae help a grasshopper find food, shelter, and a mate.

Beyond the head is the grasshopper's thorax. This body **segment** houses the muscles that power the grasshopper's movements. Three sets of legs connect to the thorax. Each long, jointed leg ends in a claw.

A grasshopper can travel ten feet per second (3 m/s) with the help of its springy hind legs.

The third set of legs is the largest. These long, muscular legs help grasshoppers jump. And jump they do! The hind legs can launch a grasshopper 20 times its body length.

Toothlike ridges line the grasshopper's hind legs. These are used for singing! Male grasshoppers rub the ridges on their legs against their wings. This action is called stridulation. It makes the loud noises that grasshoppers are famous for.

A GRASSHOPPER'S BODY

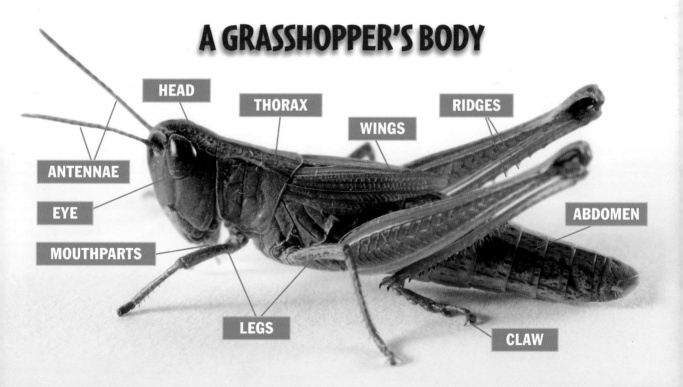

HEAD

THORAX

WINGS

RIDGES

ANTENNAE

EYE

ABDOMEN

MOUTHPARTS

LEGS

CLAW

Grasshoppers can be powerful flyers. Some African species have even flown across the Atlantic Ocean to reach the Caribbean islands!

Most grasshoppers also have two sets of wings connected to the thorax. The forewings make up the first set. They are thick and leathery. Often, the coloring of the forewings helps grasshoppers blend into their surroundings. The forewings also form a protective covering over the second set of wings.

The hind wings make up the second set of wings. These are delicate, with small veins running through them. Often, they are brightly colored. The hind wings are the flight wings. They provide most of the power needed to get a grasshopper into the air.

The abdomen is the grasshopper's third and final body **segment**. It is also the largest of the three segments. That is because it houses most of the grasshopper's **organs**.

INSECT EARS

Did you know that grasshoppers have ears? It's true! Grasshoppers are among the insects that hear with organs called tympana.

Grasshopper ears are not found on the head like yours are. A short-horned grasshopper's ears are located on its abdomen, just above each hind leg. A long-horned grasshopper's ears are located in the knees of its first pair of legs!

Grasshopper ears don't look like yours either. Instead, they resemble the eardrums you have deep inside your ears. These thin membranes vibrate when even the tiniest sounds are made.

The Inside Story

Inside a grasshopper's body, many systems are hard at work. Like other insects, a grasshopper does not breathe with lungs. Instead, its respiratory system uses spiracles and tracheae. Air enters a grasshopper's body through holes called spiracles. Inside, tubes called tracheae connect to the spiracles. These tubes deliver air throughout the grasshopper's body.

Grasshoppers also have an open circulatory system. This means that a grasshopper's blood does not flow through veins. Instead, it flows freely through the grasshopper's body. Grasshopper blood is called hemolymph. The grasshopper's heart is a long tube. It helps pump hemolymph from end to end.

A grasshopper's nervous system consists of a brain and **nerves**. Clusters of nerve tissue called ganglia make up the simple brain. Nerves extend from this brain throughout the grasshopper's body. Together, the ganglia and the nerves help control the grasshopper's movements and **organs**.

BUG BYTES

One of the world's largest grasshopper species is Tropidacris latriellei of South America. It may grow more than four inches (10 cm) long!

A grasshopper has ten pairs of spiracles. Eight of these pairs can be found along the grasshopper's long abdomen. The other two pairs are located on the thorax.

Transformation

A grasshopper's life cycle has three stages. These are egg, nymph, and adult. The process of going through these stages is called incomplete **metamorphosis**.

When a male and female grasshopper mate, the life cycle begins. First, the male grasshopper sings a tune to attract his mate. This usually occurs during the warm months when grasshoppers are active.

After mating, the female grasshopper finds a place to lay her **fertilized** eggs. She usually chooses a place in soil or plant debris. There, the female digs a hole using her pointed **ovipositor**. With her ovipositor still in the ground, she deposits the eggs into the hole.

Next, the female grasshopper covers her eggs with a sticky, foamy substance. This substance coats the eggs so they form a single cluster. Then, the substance hardens into a protective casing called an egg pod.

BUG BYTES

Depending on her species, a female grasshopper lays between 500 and 600 eggs in her lifetime.

Grasshoppers spend most of their life span as eggs in pods. This long stage of development can leave a grasshopper exposed to danger. For example, eggs develop during the coldest months of the year. However, the egg pod provides protection against the cold weather.

Most grasshoppers lay their eggs in soil. Others hide their eggs under grass clumps, on leaves, or in plant stems or twigs.

When the weather warms, the eggs hatch. This begins the nymphal stage. Between 10 and 200 tiny grasshoppers may emerge from the pod. These nymphs dig their way out of the ground. They look like their parents, except they do not have wings.

The nymphal stage is filled with growth. Nymphs eat and eat and eat. All this eating provides the energy needed for their rapid development. In fact, nymphs grow so fast that they burst right out of their skin! This process is called molting.

When the nymph's exoskeleton gets too tight, it splits down the back. Luckily, a new, larger skin has already grown underneath.

LIFE CYCLE OF A GRASSHOPPER

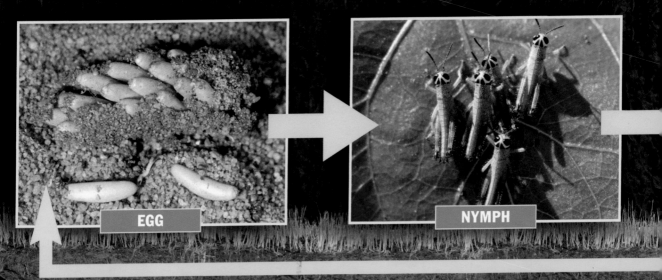

EGG

NYMPH

Nymphs molt three to five times before reaching their adult size.

In the adult stage, grasshoppers have fully grown wings. The wings are soft at first, but they harden quickly. At last, the adult grasshoppers get to spread their wings and fly.

The adult stage is short. It lasts just long enough for grasshoppers to mate and lay eggs. Their life cycle is complete by the time the weather turns cold again.

ADULT

Sunny Homes

Grasshoppers can be found almost everywhere in the world. They prefer warm climates. But they have been found in snowy places, too. In general, grasshoppers can be found anywhere there are plants to eat. That is because eating is a grasshopper's favorite way to pass the time.

Lying in the warm sun is a grasshopper's other favorite activity. So, grasshoppers are uncommon in rain forests and other thickly wooded areas. That is because the high trees in these places block out the sunlight.

In addition, a shaded forest floor cannot produce low plants. However, a break in the trees means sunshine and plenty of food. Most likely, grasshoppers will be there!

Plains and fields make ideal locations for grasshoppers. There, short plants grow plentifully. Grasshoppers can easily reach these snacks. In addition, short plants don't block the sun. These are the perfect places for grasshoppers to do their two favorite activities.

BUG BYTES

In some places in the United States, grasshopper populations can grow very high. When this happens, more than 1 million grasshoppers could occupy an area of land the size of a football field!

The family Acrididae has about 10,000 species. Of these, more than 1,000 exist in the United States.

Favorite Foods

Favorite crops include corn, wheat, and barley. Grasses, leaves, and flowers are also favorite snacks.

By now, you know that grasshoppers love to eat plants. Short-horned grasshoppers are herbivores. These orthopterans may chase humans in the movies, but don't worry. In real life, they stick to a plant diet!

Grasshoppers eat a wide variety of plants. Some species stick to one plant family or even one specific plant part. Other species eat just about any plant in sight. If you see a bare plant, it has probably been visited by a grasshopper.

Katydids and other cousins of true grasshoppers are omnivorous. They eat dead insects and animal matter as well as plants. There

BUG BYTES

Many grasshoppers eat plants that are toxic. These plants may turn the grasshoppers bright colors.

Like short-horned grasshoppers, most long-horned grasshoppers eat plants.

are also carnivorous orthopterans. Some cricket species even eat their own relatives!

Everything a grasshopper eats must pass through its **digestive** system. First, food enters the foregut. This includes the grasshopper's mouth and throat. From there, food travels to the midgut, or stomach. In the midgut, food is digested and absorbed. Then, waste is released from the hindgut.

Beware!

Most grasshoppers are plant eaters, but many other animals are not. What does this mean? Grasshoppers make a tasty treat.

Some African grasshopper species blow foam through their spiracles.
The foam contains chemicals that are harmful to predators.

Snakes, spiders, birds, and beetles are just a few of their enemies.

Grasshoppers have several ways of avoiding predators. Their first option is to do nothing! Many grasshoppers use camouflage to blend into their surroundings. By standing perfectly still, their predators will not see them. Instead, these enemies will pass right by.

If they don't luck out this way, grasshoppers can use their powerful legs to jump away. This sudden movement startles insect predators and even humans. Grasshoppers add to the surprise by flapping their wings.

Grasshoppers have a few other tricks to protect themselves. Some species spit a dark liquid at their attackers. Others ooze an unappetizing foam from their bodies. Who would want to eat that?

BLENDING IN

GRASSHOPPERS COME IN A VARIETY OF COLORS AND PATTERNS. THIS HELPS THEM BLEND INTO THEIR SURROUNDINGS. FOR EXAMPLE, SOME GRASSHOPPERS HAVE SPOTS THAT RESEMBLE CERTAIN LEAF PATTERNS.

OTHER GRASSHOPPER SPECIES MAY USE BOTH COLOR AND SHAPE AS CAMOUFLAGE. SOME SLENDER GRASSHOPPERS RESEMBLE THE BLADES OF GRASS THEY CLING TO. GRASSHOPPERS THAT LIVE IN ROCKY OR SANDY AREAS ARE OFTEN GRAY OR BROWN. THE ROUGH BODY SHAPE OF MANY OF THESE SPECIES ALSO HELPS THEM BLEND IN.

Grasshoppers and You

Many people have reasons to wish all grasshoppers would be eaten. This is because grasshoppers can be real pests, especially to farmers. You read earlier that grasshoppers eat vast amounts of nearly any plant. Unfortunately, this includes crops.

Years ago, swarms of these insects attacked fields without warning. Farmers were helpless to stop them. Year after year, grasshoppers devoured crops that would have fed thousands of people.

In 1874, the largest swarm ever recorded in the United States caused $650 million in damages to crops. The swarm of Rocky Mountain grasshoppers invaded an area 1,800 miles (2,900 km) long and 110 miles (180 km) wide. That is almost twice the size of Colorado!

BUG BYTES

Of all the insects eaten by humans, grasshoppers are the most widely consumed in the world.

Luckily, most grasshopper species live in a solitary phase. This means they do not swarm. Instead, they live alone. However, a few grasshopper species sometimes shift into a swarming phase. Then they are called locusts.

Locusts are found throughout the world. Yet there are only about nine kinds of these grasshoppers.

Colorful painted grasshoppers range from northern Mexico to the foothills of the Colorado Rocky Mountains. They are also found from Arizona to Texas.

Entomologists know that locust swarms form after a large number of females lay their eggs close together. When the eggs hatch, the new grasshoppers remain together. In North America, Rocky Mountain grasshoppers are the only species known to shift from the solitary phase into the locust phase.

Currently, **pesticides** are used to control grasshopper populations. This has greatly reduced the number of destroyed crops. However, many pesticides create other problems. Some are harmful

BUG BYTES

A single locust can eat its own weight in food in just one day!

Grasshoppers are fascinating creatures to study. Are there any orthopterans hiding in your backyard?

to the **environment**. Others are harmful to humans. Therefore, the search for a better grasshopper control continues.

Not everyone dislikes grasshoppers. In some **cultures**, grasshoppers are cooked and eaten regularly. Other cultures consider certain orthopterans a lucky sign. And, many people enjoy the sounds of grasshoppers on a summer night. So the next time you see an orthopteran, consider yourself lucky and enjoy the music!

Glossary

culture - the customs, arts, and tools of a nation or people at a certain time.

deafening - very loud or noticeable.

digest - to break down food into substances small enough for the body to absorb. The process of digesting food is carried out by the digestive system.

entomologist - a scientist who studies insects.

environment - all the surroundings that affect the growth and well-being of a living thing.

fertilize - to make fertile. Something that is fertile is capable of growing or developing.

metamorphosis - the process of change in the form and habits of some animals during development from an immature stage to an adult stage.

nerve - one of the stringy bands of nervous tissue that carries signals from the brain to other organs.

organ - a part of an animal or a plant that is composed of several kinds of tissues and that performs a specific function. The heart, liver, gallbladder, and intestines are organs of an animal.

ovipositor - a female insect's egg-laying tube.

pesticide - a chemical used to kill insects.

segment - any of the parts into which a thing is divided or naturally separates. Something that is divided into or composed of segments is segmented.

suborder - a group of related organisms ranking between an order and a family.

How Do You Say That?

Acrididae - ah-CRIHD-ih-dee
antennae - an-TEH-nee
Caelifera - kay-LIH-fuh-ruh
camouflage - KA-muh-flahzh
chitin - KEYE-tuhn
Ensifera - ehn-SIH-fuh-ruh
entomologist - ehn-tuh-MAH-luh-jihst
ganglia - GANG-glee-uh
hemolymph - HEE-muh-lihmf
metamorphosis - meh-tuh-MAWR-fuh-suhs
nymph - NIHMF
ocelli - oh-SEH-leye
ovipositor - OH-vuh-pah-zuh-tuhr
stridulation - strih-juh-LAY-shun
Tettigoniidae - tehd-uh-guh-NEYE-uh-dee
tracheae - TRAY-kee-ee
tympana - TIHM-puh-nuh

Web Sites

To learn more about grasshoppers, visit ABDO Publishing Company on the World Wide Web at **www.abdopublishing.com**. Web sites about grasshoppers are featured on our Book Links page. These links are routinely monitored and updated to provide the most current information available.

Index